THE COMMON SENSE

—GUIDEBOOK TO—

MASTERING YOUR MONEY

**Critical Skills You Should
Have Been Taught As a
Kid...*But Never Were***

ROBIN DA VINCI

Visit the Official Website at: robindavinci.com

Printed in the United States of America
First Printing: October, 2019
Robin Da Vinci

ISBN: 978-0-578-54470-0

Robin Da Vinci, Inc. books may be purchased for educational, business or sales promotional use. Special discounts are available on quantity purchases. For more information, please call or write.

Telephone (310) 399-1144; Email: robin@robindavinci.com

For orders by U.S. trade bookstores and wholesalers, please contact Robin Da Vinci, Inc. at the phone or email address listed above.

Table of Contents

Disclaimer

The Publisher has strived to be as accurate and complete as possible in the creation of this book. This book is not intended for use as a source of medical or psychological advice. All readers are advised to seek services of competent professionals in the medical field.

Readers are cautioned to rely on their own judgment about their individual circumstances to act accordingly.

While all attempts have been made to verify information provided in this publication, the Publisher assumes no responsibility for errors, omissions, or contrary interpretation of the subject matter herein. Any perceived slights of specific persons, peoples, or organizations are unintentional. This book details the author's own personal experiences and opinions. The author is not licensed as a psychologist, or psychiatrist.

The author and publisher are providing this book and its contents on an "as is" basis and make no representations or warranties of any kind with respect to this book or its contents. The author and publisher disclaim all such representations and warranties, including for example warranties of merchantability and educational or medical advice for a particular purpose. In addition, the author and publisher do not represent or warrant that the information accessible via this book is accurate, complete or current.

Except as specifically stated in this book, neither the author or publisher, nor any authors, contributors, or other representatives will be liable for damages arising out of or in connection with the use of this book. This is a comprehensive limitation of liability that applies to all damages of any kind, including (without limitation) compensatory; direct, indirect or direct, indirect or consequential damages; loss of data, income or profit; loss of or damage to property and claims of third parties.

You understand that this book is not intended as a substitute for consultation with a licensed medical, educational, legal or accounting professional. Before you begin any change in your lifestyle in any way, you will consult a licensed professional to ensure that you are doing what's best for your situation.

This book provides content related to educational, medical, and psychological topics. As such, use of this book implies your acceptance of this disclaimer.

Foreword

What is the hardest topic to discuss with others? What is the hardest topic to think about?

What is the hardest topic to make decisions about? For many of us, the answer is "money."

For many years, I have been teaching people how to succeed in their lives, launch and build businesses, and become financially successful. In this time, I have learned that personal growth and financial growth go hand in hand.

I did not get a solid financial education when I was growing up. My parents didn't know how to teach me, because their parents didn't have the knowledge or ability to teach them. Many people can relate to this.

So where do you go for this kind of education?

This book is a rare chance to look at the world through the eyes and mind of a "financial organizer" — someone who has spent decades organizing the finances of every kind of person you can imagine, from young to old, happy to sad...and from rich to poor.

Robin has more real-world financial experience than a hundred average people put together. But what makes her particularly valuable to study with is the fact that she is one of the highest quality human beings that you will ever meet. She is surrounded by family and friends at all times, which speaks to her ability to build relationships and support other people.

She has overcome more hardship than most, built a business that's more successful than most, and created a family that is closer than most. I have known Robin for almost twenty years now, and I can say that she is one of the finest people I know. She's someone I trust completely.

This book is a new way of looking at life, success, and money. Take it seriously. It can really change your life.

— Eben Pagan

Mission Statement

With each page of this book comes a promise to move you away from your "discomfort zone" into a zone that will create a real sense of clarity and comfort. You won't just get through your day; you will enjoy the day and breathe a bit easier.

Thank you for inviting me to take this journey with you. We all have blind spots and emotional triggers around money, and no matter what your financial status or your goals, you need to start from those roots in order to achieve success, and in order to be in that process you will have to move through your discomfort zone and engage with some tough questions before you can reach your financial comfort zone.

Preface

You will hear me speaking a lot about "finding your inner bookkeeper." We all have one. You will also read that I believe emotional triggers from childhood create serious issues with spending as we grow up and start our own lives away from our childhoods.

What keeps us from finding our inner bookkeeper is fear... fear that we will not be good at it, or worse...that we will fail. It is not possible to fail, and I am here to tell you why. Any forward movement is a win.

In fact, the first step is just getting started with some simple organizational methods — skills that will stick with you and give you peace of mind and some truly mind-blowing joy at the same time. In this book, we are going to bust the "Math Myth" wide open. There is nothing magical or mystifying about tracking and organizing your cash. You can **connect with your cash** in a very meaningful way. Our disconnect from the money we earn and spend is arguably the single largest problem with our world today. Everyone (well, almost everyone) is scrambling to make ends meet. Even the wealthiest among us have their challenges.

I will share this quick story: A friend comes to me after a divorce clutching unopened bank statements and dozens of bounced checks. The spouse was the one who had handled the finances and this friend was totally in the dark. In just a few hours, we opened the mail, started a simple check register, and created a budget for the month's expenses. None of these simple steps had been done before. My friend left with a bit of a smile and some weight lifted off their shoulders. Boom. Not math really, just looking at your money...with a plan! A success story to be sure.

There are many books out there that will guide your growth in your investments, tell you how to manipulate your 401k, and offer strategies to help you build your portfolio, but the tough reality is, most people do not have retirement plans and 401ks and investment and stock portfolios. The average person may have a small savings account, if they're lucky, and live pretty much from paycheck to paycheck.

If this is your reality, if you feel like a forgotten person, you are not alone. Millions and millions of us have felt disenfranchised from this whole system for most of our lives. We have never fit into the system that says we should have this amount saved by age thirty, and then that amount by forty, and oh my goodness, where we should be by age sixty-five!

I call it a "system," but it appears to be a pretty shaky system at best. When so many millions can't join it or feel left out of it or don't even know what the system really is, you have to wonder about its value. Trying to "fit" is an age-old problem and a day-to-day dilemma for most of us. It is an emotional journey with many twists and turns, but it can also be a great big learning experience if we choose to embrace it.

So here's the scoop:

Despite what you hear, there is no one system that works. That is the real myth. There is no formula that works for everyone. How could there be when your system is based on a combination of your life experiences (especially during your formative years), your determination to jump in and take control of your money, and how comfortable you want to feel about what you have and where you are in your journey? We are success stories in our own right, yet no one tells us that.

My book will help you create your own unique system by searching for and embracing the inner bookkeeper part of your brain that has caused fear and anxiety...until now! It is totally cool to be your own cheerleader for this journey. If you won't, who will be? Oh, that's right, I will too. Right there with you. Let's make this happen!

Introduction

I have always been a worrier, a great big mess of a worrier. Maybe it happened in the womb, but I remember that as early as my sixth birthday, I was worrying about the money my family did not have, lying awake at night fearful that we would wind up out on the street and hungry. I now understand that the fears and anxieties that originated with my very humble beginnings have directed my behavior toward money ever since.

All of us have foundational experiences that affect every single level of our development. You take these foundations with you wherever you go. You live with them and make them a part of every decision you make: what to buy, where to live, what to drive, and how to share your life with others…and…share your relationship with money, no matter how damaged and confusing it might be.

Taking the time to reflect on your relationship with money, and how it started and when, will help you see more clearly what is happening in your current financial picture. The confusion, anxiety, and fear are deeply rooted in your early years. You cannot move forward unless you are willing to go back and embrace when it all began. Everyone is affected and everyone is part of the problem.

We moved from the Midwest to Los Angeles when I was seventeen months old. My father had lost his job and my parents had two choices: move back to Illinois or head west to California. My father had some family in California and my mother did not want to spend one more winter in the Midwest, so off we went.

My father had had several "outside of his marriage vows" relationships, and this move was clearly a way for them to run away from their personal and money woes. A fresh start in California was just what they needed — and my brother and I were too young to have an opinion. When we got to California, though, our life did not take shape as hoped. My father did not change his behavior, and my mother became pregnant with my sister. My mother fell apart.

Rent was pretty high in southwest Los Angeles, and my parents were having a hard time making ends meet. I vividly remember being scared when they would start to fight, and the fighting was always about money. We were already struggling, and now we were going to have another mouth to feed.

I can recall arguments about money nearly every day after

my sister was born. I loved my sister from the moment I saw her, but her arrival seemed like the beginning of the end for my mother and father, and the start of a vicious cycle of anger, violence, and fear. My mother had worked hard to lift herself from a bare-bones childhood to a comfortable life before my father came along, and as their lives began to fall apart, our "on the edge" existence triggered a lot of deep and dark emotion in her. Before I was five years old, the violence had begun and worrying became my way of life.

My father started traveling for business. There were vague references as to what he was doing, but it never produced any income for our family. While there was no explanation for how my mother covered expenses in his absence, I got the sense that her family was helping. Two of my father's brothers lived in California, and one brother in particular seemed to come to our aid and bring groceries. This uncle was my favorite and I felt safe when he was around. I am also pretty certain that he helped pay the bills during my father's "away time."

When both my father and my uncle were absent, I was the object of my mother's anger and fear, and I learned very quickly what the trigger points were for her violent reactions. She was deeply embarrassed by having to ask for help, and she struggled with the absolute knowledge that my father felt no responsibility to her or his children. Whenever he was actually home for a bit, or calling from his travels, they would fight bitterly and always —

always! — about money.

At only six years old, I was already doing without so we could eat. I was putting green stamps in books and saving coupons, walking everywhere locally because we could not afford gas for the car, and learning what everyday necessities cost. I knew what the doctor would cost if we had to get our booster shots or, heaven forbid, got sick.

We had no money for extras, and if something went wrong, my mother would explode, throwing me against walls, dumping food on my head, and beating me for showing any emotion during her bursts of violence. Fear of failure and of others' opinions kept us living this way in secret…a pleasant little family to the outside world, but living in fear every single day. Some of these events haunt me to this day.

When I was nine, I started to babysit for my sister. My mother had gotten a job as a bank teller at a local savings and loan, but she could not afford the luxury of $5.00 per week for a babysitter to watch us after school. When my father came home from one of his lengthy business trips, he had a fit that she had gotten a job. I remember the fight so clearly, and being so afraid of what would happen to me once he walked back out the door.

As always, my mother took her anger out on me. I often thought that she would kill me during one of her rages, but afterward she would calm down as if nothing had happened.

Until the day she died, she never acknowledged the violence, apologized, or told me that she loved me. This disconnect took me many years of therapy to forgive, and it has had a huge impact on the way I've lived my life — and, unsurprisingly, on my relationship with money.

You know that oh-so-lousy place that makes you want to run and hide, scream at the top of your lungs, and take a sledgehammer to a wall? I have been there. I had always prided myself on being comfortable and directed in the real world, but at some point I found myself with three small children and $23.76 in my checking account, awake, it seemed, twenty-four hours a day worrying and spinning. So much so, in fact, that I ran myself right into a nice little illness and a hospital visit. I got by with some help from my family and friends, but it took getting sick to get me to take a second look at what the hell I was doing and why.

Growing up, I had an inner calculator that never led me astray. More than being physically drained and mentally fatigued, I was emotionally disconnected. Disconnected from my money, my beliefs about myself, and my beliefs in the world I had created. But with a little hard work, I was able to relocate my inner bookkeeper and regain my financial comfort level — and so can you.

I have spent years learning about emotional triggers and how they can control our lives. Money is the single largest trigger for many of us. Even love cannot overcome the fears, misconceptions, and knee-jerk reactions around it, yet in many families, no one speaks to the children about money.

No one steps into our development to insert some sanity. In my house, the relationship with money was one of silence or violence. What was yours? How did your parents handle the subject? Was it uncomfortable? Was it helpful or informative? I have not met many who have anything positive to say about their family's relationship with money. But the good news is, with a little effort, you can overcome your history and your money-related triggers to take control of your financial health.

My story is not unique, but I share it because it is relevant in today's climate of shame and fear — relevant in that it is a story of survival, of determination to change a dangerous cycle and choose a new direction. Understanding what triggers you to doubt your success, and learning to believe that you *can* succeed, is all part of the process.

How dare anyone tell you that you are not a success! If you are working hard, taking care of yourself and a family, and being a great friend and family member, you already are a success. If money is all that determines your self-worth and self-esteem, then we have a boatload of work to do.

This book, like my own story, is about doing the tough work to figure out what your relationship with money is and where it came from. How was it formed? Were you even aware you were being influenced by your surroundings and your family? (Probably not!)

The Common Sense Guidebook To Mastering Your Money contains the action steps you can take in order to view your relationship with money with a better perspective.

<u>You can absolutely do this.</u>

Just reading about the process gets you started on the road to success ... or at least on the road to discovery. And that discovery can lead to a larger, more positive picture and help you write your own powerful story.

CHAPTER ONE

Understanding your Financial Story

"Educators and scientists work around the clock to understand what makes us so driven to succeed financially; however, their bigger challenge is to learn why we so routinely fail."

— UNKNOWN

Sounds painfully familiar, right?

It was this sense of failure that brought me to "test coaching" sessions with a friend and colleague. The purpose of the sessions was to analyze how I could share my nearly thirty-five years of business and money management experience in a coaching scenario while working with someone who truly needed my insight. A win-win to be sure!

We met weekly for several months and worked through dozens of issues and new ways to connect with his finances. It was during one of these sessions that we came up with a formula that made sense and was challenging and fun to use. An idea was born. We had a breakthrough!

We had been discussing in several coaching sessions our emotional triggers and how they affect our financial decisions (see EQ).

We debated powerfully that it was not about intelligence, even though some of the financial decisions we were tracking were not well thought out (see IQ).

We determined together that these triggers and poor decisions created a true financial mess and required examination and planning (see FQ).

EQ + IQ = FQ was created.

To be clear, we did this for money management and financial purposes only. We did not invent the ideas of EQ, IQ, or FQ. Those who have trade-marked or patented studies and/or products for these areas get all the credit for them. I encourage you to do some further research in these areas if you are interested but, for this exercise, I present the following igniters of thought and invite you to answer the questions and start your inner bookkeeper journey.

EQ

Our Emotional Triggers

What is your immediate emotional response to a difficult money situation? Is it anger or fear? Is it denial or indifference? Can you identify where it comes from?

1. _____

2. _____

3. _____

4. _____

IQ

Our Intellectual Response

Once you navigate through the emotional distress brought on by this money issue, are you able to work through it logically and find a solution? How long does it take you to calm down and think reasonably? Did this process give you some insight for the next time you need to figure things out before a bigger conflict arises? Does the solution make sense?

1. _____

2. _____

3. _____

4. _____

FQ

The Hardcore Financial Follow-Through

With the solution in front of you, are you able to create a plan that successfully uses the solution? Can you discuss this plan with your spouse or partner or family to make it work? Do you feel supported by research or actual self-data? Can this become an action step that brings the emotional and financial crisis to a positive conclusion and in some kind of harmony?

1. _____

2. _____

3. _____

4. _____

If you answered "no" to any of these situations, you need to dig deeper. Honestly, digging deeper is often where our financial progress halts. You are not alone in halting your forward progress, but you need to understand that it is fear driven. You are smart enough and completely capable, but fear is a true roadblock. Fear causes discomfort and discomfort causes anxiety and anxiety brings confusion and confusion stops the learning. When you get into this cycle, you are blocked, which creates a standstill.

Formulating Your FQ

To download the full worksheet for this exercise,
visit: http://robindavinci.com/worksheet

> *"Too often we enjoy the comfort of opinion without
> the discomfort of thought."*
>
> —JOHN F. KENNEDY

Keeping Books is Crucial

Finding your inner bookkeeper may not be something you want to do. I have been told that it is not sexy or exciting and, at the very least, not much fun. I beg to differ! This entire book is dedicated to the exploration of your inner bookkeeper. You have one…you really do!

"NO PAIN! NO GAIN!"

COINED BY JANE FONDA

Defining the "Pain" is pretty easy: It will be the discomfort of really looking at how you view money, spend it, share it, save it, and agonize over it. Even bigger than that is the pain of analyzing how you feel about losing it, not making enough of it or, worse yet, having someone take it from you. This is a control issue that knows no bounds and causes your fears to run amok. The "Gain" is a little more subtle and can take a bit of time to see and understand its benefits. But, trust me, there will be tangible benefits.

> *"To be truly at peace and experience daily success, our emotional, mental and physical lives have to be in balance. When the gaps are too big between what we think and how we feel, we are giving doubt, fear and anxiety a place to live and thrive."*
>
> — Unknown

I give you this example as food for thought:

You are invited to a weekend in Las Vegas and you really want to go. All of your friends are going. None of those friends seem to have a financial reason for not making the trip, but you do. You are absolutely sure you do not have the funds to do the weekend trip. You have a keen awareness of upcoming bills, and your credit cards do not have much room on them for hotels and restaurants.

You have also been asked to participate in some events where you have to throw in your share of the cash required. You simply do not have it, but you are embarrassed to tell your friends. What do you do? If you review the simple formula of EQ + IQ = FQ, you will be able to understand this roller-coaster of emotions and logic and, hopefully, make the decision that is best for you and that represents your current financial picture. It is not easy.

All of us have experienced a scenario similar to the above.

I have worked with hundreds of people in all age groups and from all walks of life, and this struggle between their emotional response to the situation and its subsequent logical reality has crippled them all to some degree; however, working through it has been remarkably rewarding.

Real-Life Success Story

A prospective client called me saying that he was unhappy with his current bookkeeping service. He was getting no answers to his phone calls, his bills were not being paid, and his rents were not being collected. He felt like his finances were out of control. I accompanied him to his bookkeeper's office and found that most of his mail was unopened in a desk drawer. We laugh about it now. All I had to do was open his mail and I would be quite a cut above the former group.

Seriously, though, I did open the mail. I created spreadsheets for his rentals with complete information for communication and tracking. I opened his first set of books with accurate and up-to-date information. That was more than two decades ago, and we are still a team. He is quite the entrepreneur and has a many-faceted business model. Solid bookkeeping works for everyone, and it certainly works for him and his entire family.

Admit it: You are probably resisting the idea that your relationship with money comes from deep within you and is driven by fear. We just do not relate to that in our everyday lives.

We wake up and rush around all day, tell ourselves that we will deal with it tomorrow, and then days, weeks, months, and years go by with no discussion. No resolution. None of the hard work gets done in order to figure out what is going on. For the majority of us, these are skills we never learned at home or in school.

No matter our backgrounds, we all grow up with baggage that affects our lives in crucial ways. But it is never too late to change your direction and learn new financial skills. Tracking and understanding your daily earning and spending will change your life, and the lives of those around you.

You won't have to tiptoe around the subject of money anymore. You will be able to look your spouse, family, and friends in the eye with integrity and a smile. You will have peace of mind when you know what is going on financially and can make better decisions based on that knowledge. You may not be able to solve everything overnight, but as soon as you take the first step, you will begin to see progress. Money has been accused of being the root of all evil, but the truth is that a quality relationship with money can be a springboard for growth and change and happiness.

For Your Information

Definition of "EQ" per Collins Dictionary:

"a person's EQ is a measure of their interpersonal and communication skills. EQ is an abbreviation for "Emotional Quotient"

Definition of "IQ" per Merriam-Webster Dictionary:

"a number used to express the apparent relative intelligence of a person…proficiency in or knowledge of a specified subject"

Definition of "FQ" per Wikipedia:

"…the ability to obtain and manage one's wealth by understanding how money works"

For Your Information — Plus

"EQ-i" is a self-report intended to evaluate emotional and social functioning"

EQ-i 2.0 (and other related products) — MHS, Inc.

CHAPTER 2

Creating Your Success Story

"We don't see things as they are.
We see them as we are."

— ANAIS NIN

I have believed for a long time that we are able to reinvent ourselves at any time, but I had to grow into that belief. I wasn't raised to believe in myself or that I could change my circumstances. In my family, it was assumed that the way we were was the way we were going to stay. We were poor. My mother hated, absolutely hated it when anyone referred to us that way, but it was the truth.

She worked hard to present a different reality to the world: Our little rental house had to have a trimmed yard, our windows had to be washed and our curtains clean, and above all else, our grammar had to be perfect and our grades nearly perfect — but the things that could have actually helped us to a better life and a better financial condition were never really discussed.

How a person views their childhood and what they learn during their most formative years quite literally shapes their destiny, their future, and how they assess their successes and failures. The emotional triggers from your upbringing and the influences that surrounded you created your path to what you consider success and failure. *Don't* discount this when trying to wrap your head around your triggers, especially when it comes to money.

Identifying Your Triggers

To begin, ask yourself the following questions, and feel free to answer them out loud. It's quite helpful to hear yourself speak the answers; you may be surprised by your answers and how they sound. **Unspoken triggers can remain unresolved triggers,** and that is precisely what we want to address. Listen carefully to your replies.

- What were my first impressions of money?
- How old was I when I first had these impressions?
- Were there discussions in the house about money?
- What were the discussions about and what was the tone?

- Did I overhear arguments that I didn't understand?

- Was I included in any discussions as I got older?

- Did I feel afraid?

- Did we seem to have enough money?

- Did both my parents work?

- Did my siblings or others contribute money to the household?

- Did I get an allowance?

- Was I able to have all the things I needed?

- Was I able to have at least some of the things I wanted?

- When it was time for me to handle some money on my own, did I have any training or knowledge?

Depending on your answers to these questions, you will be able to figure out just how **your relationship with money (and, of course, other areas of your life) can be directly traced back to your early years**. By the time you were aware of money and what it is for and why it is important, you were probably on the wrong path. I know I was.

What I heard from my parents about money was either fighting or frightening radio silence. The silence was actually more frightening to me than the arguments. The silence created a fear, and that fear became a trigger. These kinds of triggers can be so deeply embedded in your subconscious that you react to them now without even realizing it or acknowledging it.

Let's see if any of the following thoughts or behaviors sound familiar (and notice, not all of them are necessarily negative):

- I don't know where all my money goes and I never seem to have enough.

- I buy things that I don't really need, but at the moment of purchase, I feel like I have to have them.

- I am very uncomfortable talking about money with my partner or spouse.

- I created a lot of debt before I ever left college and it wasn't necessary. I thought it was pretty normal to go a bit wild with spending once I left home.

- As a teenager, I had no respect for money and did not understand its value.

- I saved every dollar I got when I was young because my parents said that I should. I still try to save money whenever possible ... you know, for a rainy day or one of life's emergencies.

- I hate dealing with cash because I can't seem to keep track of it.

- I only like to deal with cash, and I don't believe in credit cards. My parents really only believed in cash.

- I enjoy money and I think I have a good balance about

spending and saving.

- I know how to determine if I need something or just want something ... I spend intelligently.

- I have never had control over my spending.

- Money gives me anxiety and I don't really keep track of it or care about it. I simply need it to live.

- Can we just not talk about it?

I think you get the picture: It's clear that our emotional responses can become real actions, for better and for worse. **Acknowledging the triggers is the *first real step*.** Next, we must face them head on.

Here's what you can do:

1. Take at least an hour to physically go back through your last month of spending. Start by creating a quiet work atmosphere. Tracking your money is a job, and you need to give it the same respect that your other tasks receive.

2. Download and print your bank and credit card statements and have them right in front of you, or at least have them right up on your screen if you can't get a physical copy. One of the old-fashioned ways to reconnect with your finances is to physically have them in your presence, rather than just a report out there somewhere in a cloud.

   I know we want to save trees (and I support that), but

we are trying to create our own grassroots movement toward really connecting and grounding ourselves. If necessary, create a simple worksheet by hand or on your computer to help you see the information more clearly.

In a recent study from Indiana University, researchers studied the brain and discovered that the areas of the brain that are associated with learning work far better when a person is asked to reproduce something that's been shown to them by freehand, as opposed to just tracing it or typing it out.

3. Go line by line, item by item, and connect with each of your purchases or expenses. Write down what it was for, and more importantly, record why you needed or wanted it. Be specific; this is really important. For this exercise, "need" means "need for daily life existence" and "want" means "you decided you deserved it or thought it was fun to have.

4. Carefully review your items. What kind of spending is the majority of your spending: Need or want? You must be totally honest and clear for this to be effective.

If you have a spouse or life partner with whom you share expenses, please sit down with them and do this exercise together. I acknowledge that it may not be easy or even possible right now to speak calmly with your partner about this. Many of us do not have the language for sharing these uncomfortable topics. This does not mean, however, that you can avoid this exercise.

You need to break down these barriers by discovering and conquering the triggers and emotions that prevent and discourage meaningful conversation and keep you trapped in fear and anxiety. There are thousands of books regarding the conflicts during conversations about money between lovers, friends, and family. The conflicts are real.

Play to Your Strengths by Developing Your Weaknesses

Think back to your school days. There were probably subjects that you liked and other courses that you hated. You would usually look forward to those classes that you liked and would do well in them, even excel. You didn't mind putting in extra work, and most of the time, no one had to beg you to get your homework done. The subjects that you preferred would get your attention. They would bring out the best energy in you, which would create some pretty cool results.

Those subjects are your strengths, areas of interest, or talents. They are easily identifiable, and you make an effort to enjoy them. The idea that we do well at the things we like is nothing new — it is the stuff of which success is made and is how we thrive. But what about the subjects you didn't like and didn't do well in, or found boring or difficult? What did you do? How did you handle it? What extra effort did you make?

"We all have a tendency to avoid our weaknesses.
When we do that, we never progress
or get any better."

— JOCKO WILLINK

You probably did as little as possible and hated every minute of it. So did I! But eventually, I discovered how much I was harming myself by thinking this way, and how much I liked getting good grades and getting rewarded by my teachers for my extra efforts. Then I began to put more time into areas of my life that caused me discomfort, and I got some damn good results. I was able to tackle and eliminate some pretty tough issues.

The feelings we often experience in adult life are no different. Why can't we do it all and do it well? Why do we put things aside so often? Why don't we pursue that which we do poorly? There are so many reasons. Here are a few:

- You are just not interested in doing things that you can't do well.

- You were punished as a kid or made to feel bad because you didn't do well.

- No one took an interest in your struggles with those tough areas of your life.

- You did not trust people enough to tell them about your struggles.

- When you were young, no one talked about the tough

stuff.

- You simply grew up without training for a lot of areas of your life.

- You didn't know what you didn't know.

- It did not seem important.

For those of us who were never encouraged to work harder at the things we didn't like or didn't do well, these old emotional constraints and our own insecurities and bad attitudes have to be addressed in order to find our inner bookkeeper and stop our emotional spending.

For starters, think about the tasks in your adult life that you hate doing or feel you can't do. Pick just one, and ask yourself these three questions:

1. **Volume:** Just how big is this project?

2. **Time:** How can you make the time you will need to work on this difficult task?

3. **Tools:** What tools do you need to make it easier? More education? Software? Outside services? Quiet time to focus?

These three steps can make all the difference when tackling a truly tough subject ... especially money, and more importantly, *your* money.

Remember, the truth about your own weaknesses can be

crappy to hear, but it can also really open up your ability to learn and even move forward in a significant way. Turning weaknesses into strengths takes a bit of courage and a lot of fortitude, but it invites great opportunities to embrace yourself and your life. You are going to laugh when you read this next sentence, but I am going to say it anyway:

You will actually enjoy turning that weakness into a strength.

Use the chart on the next page to list your five biggest weaknesses when it comes to money and issues surrounding money. For example, a person who's more impulsive is more likely to spend money that they shouldn't spend. Use the other columns to write down what you will need for turning that weakness into a strength.

Weakness	Volume (How big is this area? How much of your life does it impact?)	Time (How can you find the time to work on this weakness?)	Tools (What tools do you need to achieve your goal: education, software, focusing tools, etc.?)

Once you've filled out the chart, you'll want to apply this to your life and do the work. When you've achieved results in any of the areas, write it down in the results list below as a strength. For example, someone who is no longer impulsive is now calm or level headed. This might seem obvious, yet tracking and celebrating your progress is one of the pillars of self-improvement.

Results

1. _____

2. _____

3. _____

4. _____

5. _____

Turning Your Weaknesses Into Strengths

To download the full worksheet for this exercise,
visit: http://robindavinci.com/worksheet

Real-Life Success Story

A legal secretary in her mid-thirties came to see me because she believed that she could not pay her bills with the money she was making. She had difficulty adjusting her cash flow and allocating money for the right things. After she paid her rent, she wouldn't have any money left to pay anything else.

Together, we took all her bills and dissected them; we looked at her whole picture. We looked at her due dates and her cash flow, and I showed her how to allocate her bills to the correct pay period. Facing her cash-flow head-on did wonders for her. We determined how to best use her cash flow based on the due dates for her bills, which meant she was actually looking at her cash flow and manipulating it to get the best possible outcome.

Once we were done analyzing her monthly cash flow, we were able to get her ahead of her rent by a half-month, and she even ended up with some discretionary funds for herself and some extra money she could tithe to her church...something that was very important to her.

Weaknesses are not bad. They are simply areas that can use improvement. You can look forward to creating strengths where you think they are missing. We all know the feeling of conquering an issue that we had failed at before, or making something a bit better with just a little more effort, but we often exclude money and how to use it effectively from our lists of strengths and weaknesses. Strangely, given how important it is, money is a category that many of us simply ignore, or plan to get to later and then never do.

Maybe you are having a tough time connecting with your strengths and weaknesses. There are people in your life who are often so willing to point them out. Do you agree with them? If so, you need to find a way to believe in yourself and face your own truths.

What you need is some good old-fashioned inspiration. Finding that inspiration to create a successful financial future can be difficult at first; however, if you look around, inspiration is everywhere ... the way you do your job, the kind of family member you are, and the good friend you are. Managing your money will become one of your fabulous traits. Bring it into focus.

Dedication Creates Inspiration — or Is It the Other Way Around?

"Any job very well done that has been carried out by a person who is fully dedicated is always a source of inspiration."

— CARLOS GHOSN

Do we get inspired to do something outside our comfort zone and then become dedicated to it as the discomfort disappears, or is it just the opposite? Dedication and inspiration seem to go hand in hand, and I can see why. The emotion behind both is very much the same emotion, and its source can be hard to figure out. Personally, I think I find my inspiration in other people's dedication.

I'll give you an example: My father left my mother and her three children without any money and with a lot of debt. Though my mother had experience in banking, she had not worked since I was born. Getting a job after eight years must have been very scary…and what was she going to do with us? We were ten, eight, and four! But she made it work. She got a job as a bank teller and found us a part-time babysitter. She never missed work and was promoted regularly throughout the next eighteen years.

I still don't know how, but she managed our family on a starting salary of $300 per month, even though our rent was a whopping (by 1959 standards) $135 a month. I started babysitting at nine years old just to help contribute. My mother inspired me to work hard.

Yes, our family struggled, and my mother was violent and cruel, but there was also her impeccable work ethic. That has always been my inspiration during dark times. My mother's work ethic was just amazing!

All of us have someone we've looked up to, someone from whom we can find inspiration. When you are feeling lost and uninspired, it can help to think back to whomever inspired you and relive their dedication and the influence they had on your life. Perhaps they were simply kind when no one else was. Maybe they lent you a hand or showed you a new way of thinking. They could have been a good listener when you needed one the most.

Why is this important, and how does it relate to your emotional triggers and to finding your inner bookkeeper? Human beings are driven from a very young age to conform, to be one of the many and to avoid standing out in the crowd (unless the crowd approves of what you are doing and you can make money at it).

For most of us, that eliminates a lot of small, wonderful,

and inspirational goals and dreams along the way. The best way to squash a dream or to put out the fire of inspiration and dedication is to put a price on it. Sometimes you can't put a price on something worth doing; you just need to do it.

But our emotional triggers can come into play and cause us to self-sabotage. Most of us have self-sabotaging thoughts in our heads, and it is easy to feel small and insignificant in this world. Tapping into your own source of inspiration is a way to overcome these obstacles.

Drawing inspiration from others can help you find the inspiration and dedication you need within yourself. And who ultimately decides if you are a success? **The clear answer is that we determine success for ourselves.** The not-so-clear part, however, is how we can cut through all the crap to look at ourselves as successful. We have been conditioned to believe that a lot of money equals success. I believe that becoming comfortable and clear about your finances and your money habits is the true success story.

Real-Life Success Story

A business owner made an appointment with me because his accountant told him he needed a bookkeeper. This was the first year that his business had made a significant six-figure income. He walked through my door with thirteen unopened bank statements and a sheepish look on his face.

When I discussed with him and his business partner what they felt their strengths and weaknesses were, we realized that they were in need of a financial structure that worked. I created a real structure for them from the various spreadsheets and data. We got it all on one piece of software where they could track their income and expenses and actually have budgets. This became their first management tool.

It allowed my client to reconcile his credit cards, understand his spending, more carefully track his income, and get his taxes done more economically. It also allowed him to make sure his business was in compliance. He went on to manage dozens of employees and an incredibly successful business.

Tackling your emotional triggers can be the stepping stone to inspiration and dedication. Our money does not need to control us. We can have balance and happiness no matter where we find ourselves on the perceived "success scale." It is truly time to get inspired and dedicate yourself to finding that inner bookkeeper, before it is too late!

> *"ANXIETY happens when you think you have to figure out everything all at once. Breathe. You're strong. You got this. Take it day-by-day."*
>
> — KAREN SALMANSOHN

CHAPTER 3

Writing Your New Story

So, you've identified the emotional triggers that have been holding you back from financial success — now what? If you want to change your financial story, you need to begin by changing your mindset. You do not need to love numbers or be a math major to take charge of your financial picture.

The Math Myth and How it Messes with Your Mind and Money

"Doubt kills more dreams than failure ever will"

— SUZY KASSEM

When I was growing up, girls were not encouraged to like "arithmetic," let alone excel in it. I took that as a personal challenge — in fact, I was the first girl ever to win my school's 8th grade mathematics award. They were almost embarrassed to give it to me, and encouraged me to accept the English Award instead, which I had also won.

The principal would not allow me to receive both awards, even though I had earned them. As I reflect back on that moment, I realize it was kind of groundbreaking. How could the decision for a girl to accept 1st place in math have been so controversial?

Many of us, especially women, have a lot of self-doubt and fear around math. From an early age, we are programmed to believe that we are either good with numbers or we're not. Go back in time to your first memories of money. Was it quarters for the gum machine or an allowance every Friday? Was it your parents fighting about money and how there was never enough? Whatever your personal situation was, chances are you were never taught much about money, and so *the mystery of money and the myth about math went hand in hand*.

The truth is, you do not need to be a math whiz to take control of your money. Math is all about *logic* and *organization*, and although one or both of these words might scare you, you already have many of the skills you need, whether you realize it or not. We will explore the easy ways that you can connect with your cash and find the right path based on your triggers and anxieties. You might actually find this journey to be exciting — maybe even fun!

Let's start with all the things you already do well every day. Organizing a vacation, getting repairs done on your car, creating a beautiful garden, doing an amazing job where you volunteer, running a busy household while working at a full-time job. These are all pretty big things that require the use of the left side of your brain, that logical, organizational side that you are so hesitant to tap into because it feels uncomfortable.

The best way to get that left side of your brain working is to first envision the final result. I know that may sound odd, but if you think about math, you have to know what you're solving for before you can begin the equation. So, first, set the result you want.

What are some of the math/money goals you may have felt too anxious or fearful to try? Examples could include

- Putting some money away each month in a savings account
- Paying off a student loan
- Paying off one of your high-interest credit cards
- Moving out of your parents' home and finding a nice place to live
- Buying or leasing a new car
- Taking a small vacation
- Buying some new clothes
- Getting a dentist or doctor's appointment for something that is bothering you physically
- Seeing a therapist
- Taking your kids to an amusement park

You may think that most people are accomplishing these things easily, while you are struggling, but this is far from the truth. Millions of us struggle daily with cash flow, tracking our cash, and making ends meet. It can be hard to see that "light at the end of the tunnel," but that light — that goal, that result — is precisely what we need to see and project for ourselves. Then we simply take the steps to get there.

The key to achieving your financial goals is to break each goal down into smaller pieces. Let's take one of the wishes that almost everyone has: "I want to put some money in savings." "But I don't think I have enough to do that," you may say, "and by the end of the month, I have nothing left." Or you may continually promise yourself, "I will do it next month!" You hear yourself saying it, yet you are not very convincing.

But you can easily break this intimidating objective down into smaller, more achievable goals. Set a modest goal to start with — say, putting $100 per month into savings. Then break the $100 down into four payments of $25 and put that money in the bank first — yes, first — each week. This is easy to set up online, and doing it means your money goes into savings before the weekend hits. This simple move of saving first can be so rewarding. Don't wait until after you've paid everything else and made impulse purchases of things like ice cream or cigarettes or $5 coffees, all of which can add up rather quickly. Getting started is the key, no matter how small the amount. And no amount is too small.

Math and organization go hand in hand. You cannot do one without the other. So instead of looking at your money as only a math problem, view it as a more powerful and interesting set of equations:

Math = Organization

Organization = Discipline

Discipline = Knowledge

Knowledge = Peace of Mind

Peace of Mind = Success

Success = Money Sense

Money Sense = Time Well Spent and Managed

Time Well Spent and Managed = The New You

Money Myths and Beliefs

To download the worksheet for this exercise,
visit: http://robindavinci.com/worksheet

"I Don't Have Time for This!"

Have you ever heard the saying, "If you need something done, ask a busy person"? Busy people are often great managers of their time, and their secret is that they know how to orchestrate their days. You may feel right now that you "don't have the time" to work on your finances, but your sanity — and your financial well-being — depend on you finding the time.

We say we can't find the time or we don't have the time, but in the time it takes to say that, we could have looked up our account balance, recorded our cash spending, or even just taken a quick break. If you are not finding the time to take care of the difficult things, you are probably not finding the time for the wonderful things, either. **Creating time to handle the uncomfortable items creates an opening for the way-cool stuff, and we all need some way-cool stuff.**

Real-Life Success Story

A few years ago, I met with a young social media influencer who needed a method for recording her income and expenses but was not interested in having a set of books. I made the simple suggestion of creating monthly folders, one set for personal and one for business, and jotting down notes on the folders themselves to help her connect on a bookkeeping level with her income and expenses. This gave her peace of mind and a structure she could use to connect her social media value with her monetary value in a way that she had not done before. This allowed her to flourish and grow her business.

I am sure that you have had days when you were unable to get anything done, when you've gone to bed and struggled to fall asleep because your mind was racing with anxiety about all you had to do the next day. In these moments, you may feel like a victim of your day; like it ran away from you and you couldn't catch it.

This happens to everyone, but if it happens too frequently, you need to look at those twenty-four hours and see how you can rule them instead of them ruling you. Apart from the occasional emergency that truly causes an interruption, what in the world are we doing on all of those other days that is causing so much chaos?

Yet we can find ourselves thinking, "I had 8736 hours last year and 168 hours last week and 24 hours yesterday. Where did they go and why am I still stuck in the same place?"

"Until you value yourself, you won't value your time. Until you value your time, you will not do anything with it."

— M. SCOTT PECK (1936–2005)
AMERICAN PSYCHIATRIST AND AUTHOR

The bottom line is, if you are an active person with a job, friends, family, and a social life, you have a full plate. There is basically no room in the day for things to go haywire; no built-in down time or extra time to handle an unscheduled mess. Between the time you get up in the morning and when you go to sleep at night, you have sixteen to eighteen hours to orchestrate your day to the best of your ability. The real challenge is how to orchestrate those hours. This is not an easy task, but you can do a bit better, little by little, if you honor your time. You are important, and your time is the most valuable thing you have. It is yours to organize, play with, give away, sleep through, or waste, but taking charge of it is the best thing you can do. So how do you honor your time? Here are a few suggestions:

- **Separate your day into doable segments.** Looking at the entire day all at once can be daunting. It sends you into overload and can create turmoil. Who needs it? Instead, wake up just a bit earlier and spend a few minutes at the start of each day reviewing your schedule and thinking about the best way to get everything done.

- Once you have created the segments, **determine what are your "must do's" and your "want to's"** for each segment, and think about what you are likely to use as stall tactics. Yes, stall tactics: We all do it. We work on some useless or trivial thing to avoid doing the most important stuff.

- **Set a reminder or alarm for the "must do's."** There's nothing worse than missing a deadline; it will cause you more stress later.

When you begin orchestrating your days with intention, you'll find you have more energy, feel more relaxed, and can actually get everything done on time, and you will even have the time to check your account balances online and keep track of your financial goals.

I think the message is loud and clear: It may take some truly hard work to change from being a victim of your days to being an orchestra leader, but it is time to try. And if you orchestrate your day, you are likely also orchestrating your spending and giving it the attention it requires. If you are orchestrating your money, you have likely handled some of those emotional triggers that can victimize you and your daily life.

The Scarlett Syndrome

"I can't think about that right now. If I do, I'll go crazy. I'll think about that tomorrow."

— MARGARET MITCHELL, *GONE WITH THE WIND*

What would your success look like if you created a world with very little procrastination and discomfort?

Well, in order to succeed, you've got to keep your daily life daily. Breaking your spending down to the smallest time frame possible will keep it under control. It is about "staying in the moment" and managing the madness.

For example, let's revisit the Vegas trip with friends. Maybe some of your friends have the means to spend freely on a bachelor or a bachelorette weekend, but you don't. You are not sure what is coming for the whole weekend and you are embarrassed to ask. You throw down your credit card whenever asked, and you hit up the ATM a few times in order to contribute to the festivities;

you know, throw caution to the wind and live it up.

On the trip home, you are sick to your stomach because you have no idea what you spent, but you do know it was more than you had in your budget ... or did you even have a budget? Maybe you simply said you'd worry about it tomorrow, and now tomorrow is here.

Does this sound familiar?

Of course, some procrastination is very normal, as we all tend to do the things we enjoy and put off the things that we don't. We also have to do what is urgent. We usually have an inner rating system that determines the urgency factor, and completing those urgent tasks can be pretty satisfying. What isn't satisfying — and can be downright harmful — is to routinely promise yourself that you will complete tasks or put promised behaviors into motion and then delay or disregard your own promises.

Here are a few tricks to "curbing your enthusiasm" for procrastination:

- If the task is small enough, do it in the moment it happens. For instance: The trash is full and it needs to go out. *Go take it out now!* One little step. Each time you remove a small nagging item from your list of nagging items, the emotional reward is tangible. It is an emotional pat on the back, an "I did it." Yes, the trash will need taking out again, but it will continue to be rewarding if you do it when it should be done!

- If the task is a bit bigger — for example, folding the clothes in your dryer — and you have put it off, set your phone alarm for a reasonable moment in your day, and when the alarm goes off, get up and do it. And no snoozing!

- Even if you don't write it down (come on, we can't fix everything immediately), review what you spent at the end of each day. Make notes in your phone if need be, but however you record it, take the time to review what went on in your financial world that day ... before you turn out the lights and get comfy.

- Open your mail! Have you ever noticed that your mail seems to become more intimidating the higher the stack? Start sorting it right away, every day. Separate what is real from the junk, and in order to feel really good about this job, get a small shredder and shred the junk before you review the rest of the mail.

Have a highlighter nearby to mark due dates and account numbers or subject lines. This small step helps record the item in your brain, making you less likely to forget. Have a small basket or box nearby to keep the real mail safe, so you can take care of each item when it is due and necessary.

Now that you are using your time to kick those small items

in the ass, you are starting to work through these irritating emotional blocks and erasing some discomfort. So, so satisfying!

Stop Procrastination

To download the worksheet for this exercise,
visit: http://robindavinci.com/worksheet

Boost Your Boundaries

The need for discipline and the importance of setting boundaries go hand in hand. They actually help create each other. Here is a truly simple example: You decide you will not leave the house in the morning without making your bed, so you get up just a bit earlier to make sure that happens. Once you start making the extra time, you notice that you are making an easy breakfast and leaving for the morning a bit calmer. You also clean your dishes and put them away.

This is something you were probably asked to do when you were young yet couldn't see its importance. Ideally, the adults in your life would have taught you how to set personal and financial boundaries early on, by enhancing the good stuff, working to greatly reduce that which could harm you, and helping you develop the ability to know the difference.

For many of us, this was not the case, but we can still learn to set our own boundaries as adults. If this is challenging for you, creating very simple boundaries for your personal space is the perfect place to start, so you can eventually learn to create the larger and more difficult boundaries.

A boundary is a protection that you set up for yourself. A good boundary must be well-defined. Boundaries that are too loose aren't really boundaries at all, but if your boundaries are too tight, they can prevent you from learning new things and trying new ideas. There is a lot of room to maneuver, change, and make mistakes, and we often learn to set better boundaries by making good and honest mistakes. This is especially true where money and its use are concerned. If you don't yet have financial boundaries in place or you are confused by how to create them, read on!

The reason emotional triggers cause dangerous spending is that they are quick and can catch you off guard. But there are a few simple boundaries you can set that will really help with these triggers.

First Boundary: Never purchase anything when you are extremely happy or extremely upset or extremely anything. Emotional extremes create a weird physical reaction ... one that you may not be able to describe but that can be dangerous nonetheless. If you can put that boundary in place right away, it will save you from a lot of grief and anxiety.

Second Boundary: Create a healthy distance between you and your credit cards and debit cards. Don't save the card numbers on websites. Make sure that each purchase or transaction is deliberate and even takes a bit of work, so it gives you time to process what you are doing.

Third Boundary: Always do further research and never impulse buy. Firmly set a series of steps you have to go through in order to spend any money. Set this boundary for your whole family, if applicable. Enjoy the process and, if at the end of it you decide to spend the money, it will be because of careful research and a good thought process.

Fourth Boundary: Figure out your own issues before you leap to judge and or direct others about theirs. One of the more curious aspects of boundaries is that we often have very strict ones for the people around us, yet we cannot seem to adhere to the ones we have set for ourselves.

How can we be solving everyone else's problems, yet we can't solve our own? How do we know that someone else crossed a line or broke through a boundary, when we don't recognize the very same behavior in ourselves? It is easy to see other people's issues so much more clearly than our own.

Now, I understand that none of this is easy. Setting boundaries and sticking to them is a lifelong challenge. We move in and out of our boundaries all the time. We push the lines, jump over them, or just redraw them. That is why it is important yet difficult to create the right ones. The ones that you can stick to and live with are the ones you really need to cultivate.

Avoiding Emotional Competition

We think … we feel. There's a normal gap. We feel … we think. Another normal gap. Very normal behaviors! But when the gap between the two becomes large and more extreme, that is where mistakes are made and the emotional competition takes center stage. You need to work on your personal gap — the space between what you know is your truth (and your finances) and the big, fat, old emotions that get in your way and step all over you and your financial health.

By nature, we are competitors. But when the competitive spirit becomes emotionally triggered in a destructive way, no one wins. For example, the Olympics is a remarkable celebration of our natural competitive spirit, but uncontrolled, that same competitive spirit is what drove Tonya Harding and her team to try to eliminate her top competition by knocking Nancy Kerrigan in the knees with a baseball bat.

You will never go to these extremes, I am sure, but we see this scenario played out over and over again in smaller ways in daily life, and on social media. Moms who are more competitive than the kids on cheerleading squads. Dads who are more aggressive off the field than the kids are on the field. Parents who have aspirations for their children for things in which their children have no interest.

These examples are out there for everyone to view, but our emotional competition is often hidden and harder to detect. It is there, though, and it is trying very hard to sabotage our daily financial sanity.

Real-Life Success Story

A talented entrepreneur in his late thirties came to me because he felt he had a block when it came to his money. He was making more money than ever, but he felt like he had less than ever before. We sat and talked through his money blocks and where they came from and discussed the anger he felt at his lack of financial education.

Before we could even look at his actual numbers, we had to work through the triggers that had caused him to neglect the financial side of his life. I shared with him my own childhood triggers and my financial fears growing up, and as he began to work through his own issues, a new sense of financial freedom appeared.

He tracked his income in detail. He invoiced more frequently and at a rate that was market friendly but reflected his experience. He checked his accounts daily to better understand his spending and made significant changes. I believe that he would credit our coaching sessions with some of his current success.

Like it or not, admit to it or not, we are all financially competitive people. We want to be well thought of in our circle of friends and we want our coworkers to look at us in a positive way. Yet, **our biggest challenge when it comes to emotional competition is often inside our own family.**

Family is considered to be the most powerful dynamic for humans, which means it also has the potential to be the most competitive and destructive. While family can make you feel loved, safe, and secure, it can also do the opposite, and in many cases, family can undermine your emotional stability, which may result in actions that are pretty harmful.

This type of undermining may not always be intentional, but that doesn't make it any less hurtful. Comparing you to someone who achieves at a higher level, or causing you to doubt your self-worth, can be humiliating, yet some of us will accept this behavior from family members in rather large quantities.

Those old sayings "keeping up with the Joneses" and "the grass is always greener" have true significance when it comes to emotional triggers. For many of us, the very core of the issue is not actually about the proverbial Joneses next door; it is about our need to feel "as good as" our siblings or to have our parents view us as successful.

You probably have intense feelings about your rightful place in your family, in your friend group, with your coworkers, and within your community at large. You care about how they view you, and what they perceive to be your successes and failures. If you have children, your feelings of pride and worry about them also get added to the mix, and that competitive feeling comes roaring to the surface.

This emotional competition can cause you to buy cars you don't want, houses you cannot afford, and all kinds of other consumer crap that you believe will prove you have it all together and are as successful as the next person. Giving in to these destructive competitive tendencies can land you in your own private hell, trying to juggle the mess you have created but determined not to let anyone know you are struggling to stay afloat.

Even worse, you pass these emotional triggers on to your children, especially if you use them as unwitting pawns in the contest over grades, sports, or beauty standards. The cycle can be never-ending. Do any of the following sound familiar?

- "How can they afford that new car? We both work and we still have these old cars."

- "I am so tired of hearing about how well their son does in sports! Can't we talk about something else?"

- "Don't get any ideas about us moving to a better house. We can barely afford this one."

- "I work hard but I can never take a vacation. Why can't I go anywhere exciting?"

- "My parents like my older brother better because he is a lawyer. They never seem to care about what I am doing.

How can I make them notice me?"

- "My sister is just prettier and gets all the attention. My mom always plays favorites because of this."

- "I feel like I am in a never-ending cycle of competition and it makes me feel bad about myself. I am really tired of it and I want to give up."

- "I will never be as good as he is ... *ever*!"

If any of these do sound familiar, you need to establish boundaries about competition in order to put a stop to this cycle and to minimize the damaging emotional stress that results. Here are a few techniques to try:

1. Pick your battles. Competition in its simplest form is natural, yet you cannot engage in every battle. So pick one that really bugs you and give it a quick ten-minute analysis. Ask yourself why it bugs you so much.

2. Identify the feelings you get when this emotional battle comes up. List them either out loud or on paper ... trust me, it really helps.

3. Describe what money you have spent when responding to this emotional trigger. You will be surprised at this list.

4. Never, ever buy anything when you feel the competition cycle starting. Stay in the feelings and don't act out. It helps to have someone who can talk sense into you while

you are battling this trigger, so think of someone you can text or call when you feel slammed by that need to purchase something to make you feel better, who can remind you that you are already successful on your own merits. Someone who doesn't judge you but supports you when triggers arrive unexpectedly.

5. Compete with yourself and not with those around you. I used to tell my children, "Compete with yourself first, and once you have achieved your goals, then you can look around and see what others are achieving."

Healthy competition can create some incredible interactions and outcomes, but confidence in your own decision-making is really the healthiest first step to combating emotional spending. Set simple tests for yourself. Shoot for a solid "B."

Use the chart on the next page to write down four instances of emotional competition that are currently bothering you.

What is bothering you?	Why is it bothering you? What feelings come up?	What money have you spent due to this emotional trigger?	What can you do to let the feelings pass?

Avoiding Emotional Competition

To download the full worksheet for this exercise,
visit: http://robindavinci.com/worksheet

Once you have gone through these four questions (and remember to be honest with yourself), you should have a really good idea of where this trigger is coming from and why this is so important to you … and ideally, this should help you gain control of your spending due to emotional competition.

CHAPTER 4

Finding Your Inner Bookkeeper

As you have discovered throughout the previous chapters, we all carry emotional triggers from childhood into adulthood, and these triggers can adversely affect our relationship with money and keep us from reaching our full potential. Yet each day when we wake up, there is potential for personal growth and change. I believe firmly that **each one of us has an inner bookkeeper that has either been tapped into by now or is hiding somewhere deep inside**, ready to explode onto the scene.

So where do you begin? If you're currently not sure how much money you have or where your income is going, you need to start by simply getting organized. Do any of the following sound familiar?

- You have a few bills to pay but you don't have the time or the energy to calculate your cash flow, and you think you bounced a check.

- You need new glasses but you don't have the money for the co-pay ... at least, you don't think you do.

- Your tooth hurts, your kids need school supplies, and the car needs new tires, but you're not sure if you have room on your credit card this month.

- You owe on your school loan now because the deferment period is over, and your parents are giving you signals that it is time to get out on your own, but you can't find a job and you do not know where to go to find answers.

If this is you, you are standing smack dab in the middle of the discomfort zone, and you need to take concrete steps to harness your inner bookkeeper and find your comfort level.

- First, gather every single bit of your financial world into a big pile or basket or folder. All of it. Income, mortgages, credit cards, school loans, utilities, auto loans, personal loans, insurance ... whatever there is. If you have this information online, try to print it out. If you can't print it, get out paper and pen and list everything. If that is too old-fashioned, create an Excel spreadsheet or type up a list. You must get every single debt or payment in front of you.

- Now, separate this information into logical categories in whatever way makes sense to you. You should be able to more quickly access the information later if you determine how to file it.

- List your income for a month. Don't worry at this point about calculating gross income versus net income — just list the amount you put into checking and/or savings, into your 401k, or into the stock market ... and even the cash you hid under your mattress.

- Next, take a look at your debt at its lowest level. What are the exact amounts of money you have to pay during the month to avoid incurring late fees and getting into further trouble? In other words, what is the minimum you have to pay each month in every single category in order to get through to the next month with your integrity and credit intact?

- With that fully organized, note each payment that can incur a late fee (remember that rent and mortgages have late fees too) or that can impact your credit score. Also note which payments have grace periods and can be canceled if payment is not received.

- Now add up the income, and then add up all of those payments. Also, unclench your teeth, start to breathe, and for goodness sake, open your eyes. You are going to feel uncomfortable and maybe even nauseous. It is okay. You are already growing, changing, and finding your inner bookkeeper.

Let's be clear! Not all debt is bad debt. Once you have completed the tasks and taken a good, hard look at your finances, you have one more thing to do and only you can do it. Look at your debt. Not your food, auto, living expenses kind of debt … but your long-term, I want this out of my life kind of debt.

Does it include student loans? Credit cards with high interest and balances? A loan from a friend? A second mortgage on your home? This is when the real work is done. Determine your good debt versus bad debt. I say high-interest credit cards and that loan owed to a friend. Work on those first. What is on your list? What will you work on?

Real-Life Success Story

A few years ago, a dear friend's daughter came to live with me to attend a local university. Due to family circumstances, she was carrying a lot of credit card debt and had had to delay her dream of becoming a nurse because of that debt. Analyzing the debt, the interest rates, her cash flow availability, and her student loans all at the same time was very uncomfortable for her.

We worked through the discomfort as she revealed all her debt and how it had occurred. However uncomfortable it was for her, it was crucial that she face those feelings head on, and once she did, we were able to map out all the possibilities and get her on the road to reducing her credit card debt and financing the next level of her education. I'm happy to report that she realized her dream to become a nurse and is now in control of her finances. She faced her fears then and continues to do so.

Simple Steps to Make Credit Cards Work for You

Paying off that high-interest credit card may feel impossible, yet it can be done. The first step is to stop using the card for nonessential items. When you use the card randomly, you do not keep track and the charges add up. For example, say you are traveling and you stop to put gas in your car. That's all you really need to do. But instead, you use your card to get gas, buy some junk food and a lottery ticket or two, and then go to a coffee house drive-thru and get a $5 coffee. The gas stop that was $30 is now $57, and it all went on your card at 28.89 percent interest.

Here's the simple solution: plan ahead. Get a small cooler and thermos — even if you need to buy them, the purchase will pay for itself on the first trip. Make your coffee at home and bring it with you. Pack snacks with ice in the cooler, using food that you already have at home. The $30 gas stop is now just a $30 gas stop. Save the receipt and match it up with the credit card statement that you get online or in the mail.

Next, look at the very important interest rate and the very important finance charges. Checking in with those numbers is critical to getting the cards paid off. And, more importantly, never just pay the minimum payment. Applying that interest rate to everything you purchase before you purchase it will really show you just how much extra you are spending on those extras.

Tip: Curb your restaurant and fast food spending. Eat out less. Bring lunch. Have snacks in your car. Plan your meals. This really saves money while working on your spending triggers.

From discover.com:

"How is credit card interest calculated?

To do so, divide your APR by 365, the number of days in a year. At the end of each day, the card issuer will multiply your current balance by the daily rate to come up with the daily interest charge. So at the end of the month, the beginning $1,000 balance becomes $1013 when interest charges are applied at 15% APR."

Most of us do not pay off our cards at the end of each processing period, so our new charges are added to our continuing balance and interest is then calculated. Yes, your old balance will continue to accrue interest if you don't pay it off. Here's an example intended to give you a different view of your credit card charges.

Let's go back to some purchases you just made. If you pay them off when the due date arrives, no problem. If you don't, here's how it might look:

Purchases:

Sheets	$90.00
Towels	$32.00
Shower curtain	$27.00
Pillows	$45.00
Total	$184.00

Your new purchases, if they roll into your balance and remain there for a year or more, will end up costing you the purchases, plus tax (if applicable), plus your annual percentage rate. So, if your rate is 19 percent, those purchases cost you nearly $40 more.

Breaking Free from ATM Angst

We've all done it: confidently walked up to the ATM, put our debit card into the slot, entered our code, and then requested the cash amount we are hoping this machine can dispense to us. Maybe we need cash for a babysitter or drinks with friends, or to pay back a coworker we borrowed $40 from the week before, but we haven't checked our balance in a bit and we are not sure if certain checks have cashed or if any of our automatic payments have cleared.

So we take a deep breath, close our eyes and cross our fingers, and take a gamble that we can get the money we need right this minute to solve a problem right this minute. But what about tomorrow? And the next day? And the next week?

The ATM dilemma is only a small part of a larger problem when it comes to "eyes closed and fingers crossed" money management. The truth is very clear: If you are taking these risks with your cash at an ATM, you are likely taking bigger risks in other areas of your finances as well.

We all tend to put things off for a bit sometimes and sometimes these temporary procrastinations can even help you gather your thoughts and make a better decision. But ignoring something outright and hoping it goes away — such as a medical bill that you can't pay, a debt to a friend that you just don't address, or a tax notice you shove in a drawer and forget about — can have dangerous consequences. Avoiding these kinds of financial tasks can impact your credit score, not to mention cause stress and anxiety that place a burden on your physical, mental, and emotional health.

Where in the world does this willingness to gamble with your finances come from? It is usually deeply rooted in fear, because you were probably never trained by your family or educators to handle money, use it wisely, save it judiciously, and invest it for your future when you can't work any longer. Most of us learn about money management by the seat of our pants, which creates deep fear and anxiety about never having enough to get by, let alone enough for something fun or frivolous.

But everyone needs and deserves to know the basics when it comes to finances, cash, credit cards, and living-related expenses.

If you feel like you're flying blind, it's time to open your eyes, uncross your fingers, and take action. Here's how:

- **Budget the cash you need** ahead of time, before going to an ATM. Make sure that you have checked with your spouse or partner before removing cash from your account. Transparency and integrity are so important here.

- **Discuss your cash needs** with any person who might be affected by this cash withdrawal. See what their cash needs are and why there may not be cash to spend.

- **Always take a receipt**. This is not negotiable. That receipt can be your simple lifeline for tracking where the money went. Picture this: You go to the ATM. It is Friday night after work and you want cash for the weekend. You withdraw the maximum of $200.00. You are not sure how you will use it, but you feel good about having it with you. Then the weekend is over and you wake up Monday morning and you have only $20 left. You are searching your memory for how you spent it. Ah, that's right; you have all your receipts. Good job!

- **Write on each receipt why you bought that item.** Always look at "why" you are buying things. Having cash in your wallet or pocket can be very dangerous, and if you don't call yourself out on why you're spending it, it is harder to get that spending under control.

Answering these questions connects us more solidly to our cash spending and becomes the gateway to analyzing the rest of our spending. If you are reading this and thinking that you will never take these baby steps to control and understand your cash spending, we need to talk. Seriously ... we need to talk.

And talk we will ... about what is a trigger and, more precisely, an emotional trigger. I am going to ask you to use this example of a physical trigger to better understand. Picture yourself playing catch and one of the players only pretends to throw the ball to you and you instinctively react or flinch. Or someone gets close to your face and you automatically turn away. Someone may even question you as to why you turned away and you have to respond that you had no choice. Your body and your protective mechanism kicked in right away. Something triggered you to physically protect yourself. I am sure you understand where I'm going with this.

Your natural emotional triggers do the same thing. You cry when you're sad. You laugh out loud and sometimes can't control it. You respond to your environment, and that is normal. It becomes a bit trickier when confusion interrupts your flow and you respond to an emotional trigger with a need to spend.

Here are a few examples:

- You have a bad day at work so you go shopping even though you don't need anything. You feel guilty but feel unable to fix the situation.

76

- Your friends want to go out and your credit cards are maxed. You go to the ATM and pull out cash and spend it because you want to fit in.

- You are sitting in front of your computer to pay bills and you have anxiety, so you go onto a website and find something to buy that brings happiness for a few minutes. You push purchase because your card is on file and it's easy ... and not a good thing. Remove your cards from websites. Make it harder to spend.

I mention these few examples knowing you will relate and, hopefully, take a deep breath and realize that you can go from upset to success in a few seconds. Tackle just one at a time. First, look at the situation that starts a trigger. Now stop. These few seconds are critical. No joke. It only takes a few seconds to neutralize a trigger, and if you have taken away the easiest parts of spending, those few seconds are built for success.

Knowledge is Power

Today, it is easier than ever to connect with your cash and stay on top of your finances online, but oddly enough and sadly, many of us don't.

You have cash, checking accounts, credit cards, personal loans, and other financial burdens that stare you in the face, keep you up at night, and ruin some perfectly good mornings. When an emotional trigger becomes an unnecessary expenditure through careless or wasteful spending, you predictably go into "cover-up" mode, and then the stress kicks in and the burden becomes larger than life. Wouldn't it be nice if we could take that emotional burden and replace it with something that feels better and really works for us? Something that is more productive and requires a lot less energy to understand and process?

Real-Life Success Story

An important task for one of my clients was reviewing and identifying his credit card expenses. Creating a shared Google doc where he could see what he was spending on his business credit cards was a phenomenal leap of money management for this client. It forced him to take the time to answer the questions of who, what, when, why, and how, resulting in the realization that some of those items on his business credit cards were actually personal. We then created a Google doc for his business travel. For both business and personal expenses, the best audit defense is credible and detailed information. Great record keeping is the key to surviving an audit.

Financial sense starts with the ability to determine the "who, what, when, where, how, and why" of your cash and credit picture.

- **Who** benefits from this spending? Is it you or someone you love or someone you want to impress? Understanding who is affected by this, or who benefits from it, fills in part of the puzzle.

- **What** is the actual item you are buying? Is it an intentional choice, or are you randomly buying? You have made the decision to buy an item and have placed a level of importance on it. Now that a little time has passed, is the item still at the same level of importance?

- **When** are you choosing to buy things? This question is the toughest because you have to stop and check out your motivation and your emotional triggers. When are these spending sprees and/or unnecessary purchases happening? I am going to state this again: Do not spend money when you are extremely upset or extremely happy ... or extremely anything!

- **Where does this purchase fit into your life?** Is it urgently needed? Does it have a place? Very few people take the time to ask where an item will end up once they have it.

- **How will you comfortably pay for this item?** If you could only pay cash for it, would you be able to do it? If that answer is no, then you really need to investigate what is making you buy this item. Even emergencies should still be analyzed for the "how."

- **Why do you need or want this?** This, of course, is the ultimate question. The regret and guilt always accompany the why. Not only do you have to answer this question for yourself, but if there are others who are affected by your spending, they may be demanding answers as well. You should absolutely understand in advance what your "why" is, so you can more effectively answer the rest of the questions.

Use the following columns to write down four items or services that you are conflicted about buying. Then, I want you to go through each column and answer the questions.

Once you've answered all these questions for the specified item or service, ask yourself: Should I go ahead with the purchase?

Remember to be honest with yourself.

Who benefits from this spending?	What is the item or service you are buying?	When are you buying? (What is your frame of mind?)	Where does this purchase fit into your life?	How will you pay for this item?	Why do you need or want this?

Gaining Financial Sense

To download the full worksheet for this exercise,
visit: http://robindavinci.com/worksheet

Understanding the emotional triggers that are causing your spending, analyzing the reasons you are making the decisions, and then doing some simple math will help you make sense of your "elusive" financial picture.

Another great way to keep your financial wits about you is to break down your financial struggles into smaller pieces, looking at the smaller picture rather than the larger picture. For example, say you have leased a car and chosen the 10,000-miles-per-year option, assuming that 10,000 miles is more than you will ever drive in a year.

You are four months into the lease and you have driven over 5,000 miles, but you don't stop to do the math. Then, when the first year of the lease is over, you have used 13,383 miles of your allotted 30,000 miles for the 3-year lease, but you still don't do the math, and you end up at over 20,000 miles before year two has ended. Not a good scenario if you intended to turn in the car. What should you have done? Well, you should have done some simple math *before* you leased the car.

10,000 miles divided by 52 weeks = 192.31 miles per week

192.31 miles per week divided by 7 days = 27.47 miles per day

Do you need to drive more than 27.47 miles each day to live your life comfortably? If you do, then perhaps a lease with a 10,000-mile-per-year limit is not for you. The financial consequences for going over your mileage are substantial, and you signed a contract saying you wouldn't. Calculating your finances in this matter doesn't have to be complicated. It will show you what it really takes for you to live daily, weekly, monthly, and yearly, and can be a real eye-opener.

Now let's take that same approach to your living expenses:

Your rent is $2200 per month.

Your utilities are $130 per month.

Your car payment is $360 per month.

Your health insurance is $590 per month.

Your groceries are about $120 per week, or about $480 per month.

Your gasoline is $35 per week, or about $140 per month.

Let's do the math!

The total for the above monthly expenses is $3,900 — let's call it $4,000 per month, or $48,000 per year.

$48,000 divided by 52 weeks = about $925 per week

$925 divided by 7 days = about $135 per day

So, in this scenario, you need about $135 per day to meet your minimum requirements. The example here includes standard expenses that most of us have. Now, wouldn't you plan differently if you looked at your financial needs on a daily basis? It is so important to approach your finances this way instead of simply living paycheck to paycheck and hoping that you can cover your bills. You will absolutely change your spending habits if you look at your money as funding your daily life, rather than as something that happens twice per month.

We pack a lot into each of our twenty-four-hour days. In fact, most everything we do routinely is done daily, yet we look at our finances only every once in a while. Incorporating financial planning into our daily routine makes so much more sense. We don't need a scary money monster hiding in the shadows any more.

The Daily Integrity Session

I take fifteen to twenty minutes each day and I call it my "integrity session." I take my receipts for purchases and cash and identify them. I look at my cash accounts and record them, and I check for any credit card activity or email notices or warnings. Sometimes it takes a bit longer and sometimes not more than ten minutes.

This is the most important thing you will do with your money each day. Even if you work this into your schedule every other day, you will create simple cash flow management, a clearer understanding of your spending habits, and enormous peace of mind. I have been called old-fashioned regarding my methods, and newer generations may find it archaic, but the actual recording of cash, either in a hand-written register, on an envelope or folder, in a spreadsheet, or using a current cash-flow software, will keep you directly involved and incredibly connected with your money.

The more time you put between spending and looking at your funds, the more room you create for error and doubt and anxiety. When it comes to avoiding your money and how it is or is not working for you, time is not your friend.

Let's take a look at a few steps toward setting up your own personal "integrity sessions."

- **Create an approximate timetable for your day.** Can you start your day fifteen minutes earlier in order to review your spending? Can you create a time each evening before you go to bed? Do you have any time during your waking hours to have your "integrity sessions"?

  If you are feeling pressured by a daily look, try for at least a few times a week or once per weekend. It is absolutely imperative that you start spending some time managing your money. Once you get into the rhythm of it, you will feel incomplete if you do not do your reviews.

- **Arrange to get online access for your accounts,** both

for your bank accounts and your credit cards. Each bank and credit card is different in its setup, so it will take time to get this arranged. Once you are able to access your accounts whenever you want, a whole new world opens up.

- **Always, and I mean always, have a list somewhere of what is outstanding as far as uncashed checks, pending auto debits, and the like.** You would be surprised by how many millions of people forget they have outstanding checks or auto debits coming straight out of their cash flow. You have to account for these items daily. They make a huge difference to your worry levels.

- **Know the difference between the bank's balance and your actual balance.** The bank will only have recorded what has been presented to them. If you have items that they have yet to see, you need to subtract those items from the balance they are showing. This is the most integral part of the "integrity session" each day. The bank balance should either be higher than your balance or the same — absolutely never lower. If you show a balance higher than the bank shows, something is wrong.

- **Look for fees and finance charges.** They are charged at many different times of the month and can adversely affect your cash flow. Timing is everything. These charges can cause bounced checks and failed auto debits, and can be the difference between getting $40.00 out of the ATM and having no funds available for your use.

These daily integrity sessions will dramatically show you that discretionary funds are in your future. Now let's take a look at the real definition of discretionary funds.

Using Discretion with Your Discretionary Funds

"Discretion is the perfection of reason, and a guide to us in all the duties of life."
— WALTER SCOTT

What are discretionary funds? Millions of us have never had any, so we probably don't have a good definition. Discretionary funds are *the cash left over for you to spend "at your discretion," or based on your own judgment, after all of your debts have been paid.*

So, discretionary funds are only for the wealthy, and not for working folks with kids, mortgages, school debt, and consumer debt ... right? *Wrong!* We all have the power to have discretionary funds. We can all enjoy the pleasure of using our discretionary funds. Once you discover this hidden area of your finances, budgeting will become much less mysterious and much more practical.

Discretionary funds used to be called "mad money," because it wasn't the money you put away for a rainy day or for emergencies, it was actually money to go a little crazy with and spend on something you wanted, rather than on something you needed. There is a big difference! Mad money was money you had earned but didn't owe to anybody, so you could just have some fun with it.

Discretionary funds have now become a bit more serious. Today, lenders look to see if you have discretionary funds during a loan process. Your credit score is determined by your debt-to-income ratio, which brings into play your discretionary funds. These funds may now be needed to get your child the "extras" they need for school because so many services and supplies are no longer provided. Discretionary funds today play a vital role in your ability to have a slightly more comfortable life.

Get your credit score if you have never done so. Your first one is free. Do not sign up yet for anything else. Download it and study it. It is part of being an adult.

So how do you determine why your discretionary funds can be used, and for what? Well, I do not want to make it sound silly or insignificant, because it is very serious, but it really comes down to the "yup" or "nope" test.

Once you have gotten control of your finances and you have some discretionary funds to spend, the key is to not fall back into the trap of letting your emotional triggers drive your discretionary spending. Emotionally, we say yes or no to a lot of things for reasons that are buried somewhere deep inside us.

One clear memory I have of trying to create some discretionary funds was babysitting all hours of the day and night (at 50 cents per hour) to save enough money to buy a pair of fun shoes to go with my two non-uniform skirts. I brought the shoes home and my mother proclaimed immediately that they were the ugliest shoes she had ever seen. Can you guess what one of my emotional triggers has been for decades? Yup. New shoes bring me joy, and some of them are quite crazy-looking. Wham, bam! An emotional trigger you can see coming from miles away.

My discretionary funds will always scream for shoes when I let my emotions go unchecked. But I use the "Yup/Nope test" to find my way out of the fog and keep my spending under control. I have finally developed that filter.

What if there's an item you really want but your discretionary funds don't quite cover it? You might feel compelled to put the item on a credit card, figuring that you can pay for it in two payments, essentially borrowing from future discretionary funds. So what if there is a little interest to pay? You are now entering treacherous territory — you have just lost your bout against emotional triggers and emotional spending, and your discretionary funds have flown out the window.

Discretionary funds are those funds that are available *now*, with no consequence. You will not incur any debt, owe any interest, or have to pay for it over time. If it doesn't fit this description, it isn't discretionary spending.

So how does the Yup/Nope test work? It is as simple as answering yes or no to a few simple questions before you make each purchase. We can either take a positive approach to this or go down a negative road. I am taking the positive approach here, so you need to be able to answer a really powerful "yup" to all of the following questions before spending one single dime. Are you ready? Here goes ...

1. Are you able to spend this money **without affecting your ability to provide for your daily needs**, such as housing, food, utilities, insurance, and transportation?

2. Are you able to spend this money **without affecting your ability to pay current and/or future bills**?

3. Are you able to spend this money **without upsetting anyone with whom you share this money**, and are they in agreement with the expenditure?

4. Are you able to spend this money freely, **under no pressure from anyone else to do so**?

5. Are you able to spend this money **free of guilt and/or anxiety**?

Okay. Now you have gone through the questions and you know that you have discretionary funds. Or maybe you are not quite there yet and you have a bit more work to do. Either way, there are some steps you can take to feel better and more in control of your cash flow.

If you have discretionary funds,

1. Put all of it in a savings account period. Even if it is $20.00.

2. Put one-third away and use two-thirds to pay down debt.

3. Put half away and use half to pay down debt.

4. Spend it on something that makes your life easier ... something special.

5. Give it to someone else to make their life easier ... something necessary.

If you do not yet have discretionary funds,

1. Stop your use of the ATM ... really, you have to do so right away.

2. Stop eating out ... do meal planning.

3. Study your spending. Study all of it. Make lists. Know where the money you do have is going.

4. Stop competing with others to have "stuff."

5. Get a role model who can inspire you to a new level. We all need one. It is normal to feel defeated, but it is not necessary to stay defeated. You really can be your own hero during these struggles.

If the answers to all the Yup/Nope questions were "yup," go ahead and enjoy your discretionary funds! Congratulations, you now have a new definition of discretionary funds. It is time to spend with confidence and a smile.

Ascending to the Comfort Zone

Congratulations — if you've come this far, you've journeyed through the discomfort zone, and you're probably already feeling much better about your finances. Seeking ways to reach our goals and incorporate better money habits into our daily lives is what real potential is all about. Conquering something that scares us, delving into the unknown, creating a new scenario for spending — even a small one — is success!

You may have started this process believing that you could never find the inner bookkeeper or money manager deep inside you. But that is simply not true.

Real-Life Success Story

A young, spirited entrepreneur in the services industry came to me with his wife and little girl and said, "We're starting to make money, but we are not keeping track of our finances even though we know we need to. Please help!" Together, we created books, created a structure, got his workers on payroll, procured a workers' comp policy, created a cash flow budget, and made sure all his bills were current and had no late fees. Organized bookkeeping allowed his business to grow without worry and kept him compliant with all the regulations for the industry he was in. More than two decades later, he's still a major player in his industry.

Every time you worry about where your cash went, or if that check will clear, or when your paycheck will hit your checking account, you are tapping into your inner bookkeeper.

Every time you hesitate to spend money or put your credit card away, you are tapping into your inner money manager.

Every time you check your bank account and question a debit or make a call to your bank for better rates, you have found your inner bookkeeper.

Every time you look at your paycheck and wonder about your tax withholdings or check in with your HR person, you are working your inner bookkeeper gene.

I am certain that you are getting my point.

You have the ability and the desire to make your money managing and bookkeeping skills come alive. These skills may not look sexy or sound like fun at first, but if you even stick your big toe into the bookkeeping pond, you will begin a journey that is satisfying, rewarding … and yes, even fun.

No matter what we do for a living or our educational background or our socioeconomic label, we all use money. So why do we avoid the very life-blood of our daily life? Not knowing what's happening with your finances is torture. Trust me, knowing is better. So why are you torturing yourself? It may be uncomfortable, but the money discussion is one you need to have with your friends, your family, your partner, your children, and/or your community — and, most importantly, with yourself.

I am inviting you to join the discussion, tap into that inner bookkeeper you know you have inside, and start to figure this whole money relationship thing out. The first steps will bring peace of mind. The next steps are mind-blowing.

"A Look Behind the Curtain"

In conclusion, from my bleak childhood perspective on money to the frightening financial position I found myself in as an adult, I have experienced a boatload of cash crunching and "what's next" worries. However, I have also had the unique privilege of having a "look behind the curtain" of how highly successful and top-earning people handle their finances.

I have been right there in the trenches when enormous successes were achieved. And although the average person has very little sympathy for the plight or angst of the wealthy, I can tell you that the emotional triggers and the worries look just the same from the rich side of the $ sign as they do on the not-so-rich side.

Remember, I am talking about feelings, not actual cash. It is hard to give a rat's ass about a multimillionaire who wakes up to great cash flow and no real money worries, but when it comes to the emotional triggers that got them there or will keep them there, well, they are not so different than yours or mine.

And why is that? How could the triggers be the same? Do you realize how many people with tons of cash and investments are still disconnected from their financial lives? I have read countless stories of celebrities going bankrupt. We cannot imagine how they had so much and squandered it.

Well, this is how: They never actually understood it or connected with their good fortune. We have athletes who cannot take care of themselves once their careers have ended because they spent wildly. Why? They weren't given the tools to handle fame and fortune. It goes right back to our childhoods. We dream of money, but does anyone tell us or show us what to do if we get it? How to hang on to it?

We sure feel like failures if we don't ever have money, but having it and losing it can be just as terrifying. I have rarely read a success story about a lottery winner; some go into hiding and others are back to being broke in a few years. Again, we just are not trained to be a financial success.

I was on a plane returning from a trip to Phoenix and I was sitting next to a young woman in her early thirties with a master's degree in business. We started chatting. She had been meeting with other women across the country brainstorming how to bring new ideas to the world market and support women in business. I was so excited to be sharing this conversation with her; however, when she asked me what I work at and am passionate about, she was visibly upset at the telling of my story. Not that she wasn't thrilled or impressed, but she was angry that she had navigated more than twenty years of education without being able to navigate the simplest bookkeeping principles!

She flatly asked me, "Why didn't they teach me any of this? How did I get out of school with an MBA but without the ability to create my own business books?" I knew the answers to those questions, and throughout this first look at how I feel about this subject, I have answered a few and probably raised many more.

I can sum up my beliefs with three statements:

1. Your earliest impressions of money, before you even knew you were being influenced, dictate your responses as an adult. Believe me, you can trace these impressions back and see them clearly.

2. You need to connect fully with your cash. Money is a daily force to be reckoned with, and whether you have a ton of it or very little, being disconnected from your finances will harm you.

3. Until you own your behaviors regarding money, they will not improve. When you confidently own your financial

picture, your full picture becomes clearer and simpler.

I have years of money experience both personal and business to share. I have made mistakes and recovered from them quite a bit wiser. Why should you have to make the same mistakes if we can figure it out before it happens? I promise that you will benefit but without all of the pain (maybe some ... but not all) and you can lean on me during the experience. Finding that inner bookkeeper and moving from the discomfort zone to a more confident and clearer comfort zone does not mean you'll give up your day job and join the world of accountants and bookkeepers. What it means is that you have begun to conquer your money triggers and those math myths and many of the other "blocks" that kept you tied to a money loop from which you could not escape. Now you can! One block at a time. You can do this!

Mission Restated

I wish to spend the last third of my life (yes, I am shooting for the ripe old age of 100) sharing my experience with you. My motivation is to provoke thought, encourage knowledge, and promote you all to "bookkeepers-in-training." Don't give up your day job yet; however, be prepared to enjoy money conversations, sharing financial ideas, and passing along these values to your family, friends, and partners. They will notice the calmer, more peaceful version of you!

I want to provide some of the tools for this financial adventure. It's called putting on your big person's pants and learning what money really means! Are you pulling them up yet?

Finding Your Inner Bookkeeper

Take the Quiz

1. I keep and store my receipts for expenses either paper or paperless

   a) always

   b) when I feel it is necessary

   c) never

2. In case of a lost or stolen wallet with ID cards and credit cards, I

   a) have copies of all of them, both front and back for easy identification.

   b) have the numbers stored so I can reference them.

   c) never do either "a" or "b."

3. I check my bank accounts and credit card activity

   a) pretty much every day.

   b) once in a while but at least once per month.

   c) if I am forced to because of a problem.

4. I understand and review my credit report

   a) routinely.

   b) yearly.

   c) only when I am forced to because of a problem.

5. I can easily identify every item charged on my debit or credit cards.

   a) Yes, I check them regularly and can identify them.

   b) I check them occasionally but have to do some digging to remember some of them.

   c) No, because I do not review the charges.

6. Keeping and paying for insurance coverages is

   a) important and I have all areas of my life covered and in order.

   b) difficult but I make sure I have what is required.

   c) too expensive and I worry that I am not covered correctly.

7. I set time aside to review and manage my money

   a) at least weekly.

   b) at least once per month.

   c) rarely because I have no time.

8. When I start a project for my finances or other related projects, I

   a) follow through quickly and complete them.

   b) procrastinate a bit but finish within a reasonable time.

   c) cannot seem to finish them and feel guilty.

9. I read or watch self-help and/or inspirational topics relevant to money management

   a) frequently. They help motivate me.

   b) once in a while. I find them to be useful tools.

   c) rarely. They are not necessary or helpful.

10. My money ... my finances

   a) challenge me but I enjoy the process and the results.

   b) scare me but I get through them because they are important.

   c) worry me because I feel disconnected from them and struggle to understand them.

Score:

_____ out of 20 Points

a = 2 Points   b = 1 Point   c = 0 Points

14 -20 points = Your inner bookkeeper is alive and well and waiting to burst on the scene.

7 - 13 points = You have the skills, but you are resisting jumping in with both feet.

0 - 6 points = You are a bit blocked, but you acknowledge you have work to do and you need to dig deeper.

To take a more in depth quiz,
visit: http://robindavinci.com/quiz

Bonus Chapter

*"When we fail to communicate effectively and lose
... everybody loses.
When we embrace difficult communication and win
... everybody wins."*

— Paul Tuck, trainingjournal.com

It has been said many times and in many ways: Don't talk about sex, politics and/or religion when you are in a group of people or at a party or, in fact, anywhere if you wish to keep the peace. For me, a fourth category is right up there as number one. MONEY!

Here is the truth:

Parents do not or cannot speak to their children about money. College roommates do not or cannot discuss the simplest of money issues. Newlyweds have entered into marriage without a single conversation about budgeting and what to do with their joint incomes; not even a full conversation about who is responsible for what or if they even view money the same way. What are the boundaries?

Couples split up over money all the time. Families are torn apart by money ... the lack of it, too much of it, or what's left of it. So few of us know how to navigate the treacherous waters that surround conversations about money.

What is so mysterious and why are we so afraid?

We are afraid of what we don't know.

We are afraid of what others think.

We are afraid of being wrong.

We are afraid of being afraid.

We are human, and humans avoid what they cannot do well.

We need to jump in, and here's how. I will start with some negatives to get them out of the way.

- Do not give a loved one money without speaking to them about responsibilities. No big lectures, just speak about the exchange. This includes loans, allowances, living expenses, and fun money.

- Do not assume others understand your view of money or your history with it. Speak honestly about your relationship with money. No drama necessary but, certainly, some honest facts.

- Do not give the responsibility of your money to someone else without a clear understanding of how it will be handled.

- Do not put off difficult discussions about your finances until there is a better time. There is never a good time for a difficult discussion, but there is a right time, which is always before a mess is created.

- Do not pretend you don't care enough to understand how your finances work or if they work. It is not okay to play the indifferent card with your family or partners.

Indifference is rude and it will bite you in the ass. You need to engage fully in this area of your life or none of the other areas of your life will come together correctly.

Now for some positive reinforcement:

- Always approach a partner or family member with kindness and calmness when discussing money.

- Always prepare or write down your thoughts about what is bothering you. Be sure to prepare both positive and not-so-positive thoughts/points so your audience hears you.

- Always be an attentive listener. We often hear what others are saying only in order to formulate our own response. Just listen and let the information sink in. It is also okay to expect the same from your partner, family, or friend.

- Always be prepared for a solution with a compromise. Having it all your way, even if you can prove you are more "right," will not bring about a resolution. Compromise is not a weakness. It is smart!

I can hear you now yelling, "I have tried all of that and it does not work!" If you believe you are not getting through to your audience, you need help with your presentation and, perhaps, your overall strategy. This is where a third person, an unbiased opinion, or an expert can help. I am asking you to research and learn the language of money or the very definite art of communication in this crucial area of your life.

In my thirty-five years of bookkeeping, accounting, money management, and coaching, I learned that a balance of power and simple ground rules are good first steps. No one person should have all the power over finances, and everyone needs to follow guidelines that are fair and uncomplicated. Without a baseline of shared power and knowledge, the intimidation factor leads to arguments and misunderstandings.

I have worked with many married couples, business partners, and families, and intimidation is a weapon of mass destruction in a money relationship. We rarely come to any relationship as "true" money equals, so the balance is out of whack at the start. What you do to create a form of equity will help you start your relationship off on the right foot.

Who doesn't want this on track from the very beginning? If you don't, why not? What triggers are holding you back? Maybe we should list a few triggers that we learned in previous chapters and see if we see ourselves following a distinct and decidedly difficult and destructive pattern.

I feel it is the right time to reiterate that I went to therapy often during a thirty-year period to address each and every trigger that caused me to self-sabotage or run away from an issue. I talked about my fears regarding money and the lack of it as motivators for some downright bad decisions.

About the Author

From major industry players who need accounting and business structure to students in debt... Robin has helped them to get their finances, and more importantly, their emotional triggers surrounding money... in order.

With thirty-five years in bookkeeping, accounting, and financial management, Robin has more real-world financial experience than a hundred average people put together. Robin came from very humble beginnings and had to develop her own financial and emotional well-being. It is because of her journey, that she is prepared to help you overcome the obstacles you'll face in your journey.

Thanks to the help of Robin and her teachings... people from all walks of life have been able to flourish financially and personally. She has been able to help entrepreneurs' businesses to thrive. She believes in teaching students how to get out of debt and plan for the future. She advises and encourages businesses on how to stay in compliance... which allows them to grow their businesses and play to their passions and strengths. And she assists major industry players to not only get their books in order... but also guides them through the emotional barriers surrounding money which prevents everyone —rich or poor— ultimately, from achieving success.

Additional Resources

http://robindavinci.com/index.php/resources/

This link includes:

Form 1040 Schedule C Tutorial

Form W9 Tutorial

Form 1040 EZ Tutorial

Form 1040 ES Tutorial

Form W4 Tutorial

Form W2 Tutorial

Form 1099 Tutorial

Form I9 Tutorial

How To Plan Your Paycheck Video

IRS Tax Withholding Calculator